MY BLACK ROSE HAS TURNED RED

BY CECIL OYOO ACHOLA

MY BLACK ROSE HAS TURNED RED

It's another morning,

But today I'm not mourning,

My soul is smiling,

My heart is flying,

Out of my chest,

Today I'm at my best,

What a nice feeling,

A feeling that has brought to my heart a permanent healing,

Finally, my black rose has turned red.

<u>LOVE</u>

Love is a black sky,

And in it now I fly,

But I have no wings just a small heart,

I'm afraid I'll fall and get hurt,

Hold my hand and don't let me go,

For even if I'm scared,

I still want to fly because I love this black sky.

<u>WHY DO YOU GET BLUE?</u>

Why do you get blue when I say it?

Yet you worry so much when I don't eat,

Why do you get blue please I need to know?

Yet you have never said NO.

SWEET SONG

You are my one sweet song,

Yes, my love you are,

My heart warms at your tune,

My soul smiles at your flow,

You make me glow,

My one sweet song,

Yes, my love you are,

My mind melts at the thought of you.

<u>YOUR HEART IS A BIRD</u>

I'm under this tree,

Still waiting for it to be free.

Like a Lion I won't leave,

For without it I can't live.

Dry leaves fall on me,

But still here is where I want to be.

I'll wait till it's out of its nest,

I'll wait although your heart is a bird.

<u>**I MISS YOU**</u>

Days have passed,

So many hours that I've cursed,

This distance that I badly hate,

Is keeping me apart from my soulmate.

How much longer must I wait?

How much more of this can I take?

How many more smiles can I fake?

I wish you knew how much I miss you.

ARE WE OK?

Are we ok, please I want to know.

The beautiful smiles are gone,

An unusual face has been born.

Suddenly my jokes aren't funny,

And you call me by my name not honey.

Are we ok, please I want to know.

I'M BLEEDING TEARS BECAUSE OF YOU

I had no fears but now I do,

I'm bleeding tears because of you.

<u>**I'M TIRED OF BLACK AND WHITE**</u>

I miss the YOU I used to know,

Maybe you said yes when you meant NO,

I fell for white,

But now it's not quite.

Where is this black coming from?

I'm tired of black and white.

<u>**MAKE ME PART OF YOUR BEAUTIFUL SOUL**</u>

Please make me part of your beautiful soul,

For It's not enough that I love you.

And It's not enough that you love me.

I want more for you,

I want more for me.

A deep connection,

A perfect imperfection.

Please make me part of your beautiful soul,

From deep down let's relate,

Let's do this before it's too late.

Please make me part of your beautiful soul,

For it's not enough that I love you,

And it's not enough that you love me.

I want more for you,

I want more for me.

<u>TEARS</u>

What's sweet about love when it's all tears?

My heart is weeping,

Sobbing in pain,

A bleeding heart,

What's there to gain?

What's sweet about love when it's all tears?

I LOVE ME TWICE

You are a dove,

You, my only love.

My love for you is deeper than the ocean and the sea,

So deep that only our souls can see.

I love you so much and you know it,

But I won't lie that because of you I don't eat.

Don't confuse love for foolishness I'm still wise,

My love, I love you but I love me twice.

I DON'T WANT THIS LOVE TO BE OUR LITTLE SECRET

Why are you afraid?

Why don't you want them to know?

I don't understand why we have to hide,

Is it my side or your side?

Please tell me why,

For I'm tired of saying this lie.

I don't want this love to be our little secret.

I DON'T CARE ABOUT THE WORLD

I don't care about the world,

Trust me I mean every word.

To them I'll always give closed ears,

I just want to prove my love to you even if it will take me years.

So please don't ask me what people will say,

Because I don't care about the world.

<u>**MY VEINS SPEAK OF YOUR NAME**</u>

My veins speak of your name,

But my heart doesn't want you anymore.

My blood still remembers your shame,

But my soul doesn't want you anymore.

My brain got tired of your game,

And I don't want you anymore.

My veins speak of your name.

<u>**THE HEART WANTS WHAT IT WANTS**</u>

I'm tired but I can't leave,

For without you, I don't know how to live.

My entire self wants to go,

But my heart won't let me.

With all these pains, I'll still stay,

No matter what, I won't go away.

My entire self wants to go,

But my heart won't let me.

I'm tired but I can't leave,

For the heart wants what it wants.

I HATE THAT I CARE

I care so much, but for what?

You are a free bird,

That hates to settle and afraid of building a lasting nest.

I force you to take every single step with me,

But not anymore, my love I'll let you be.

I just hate that I care.

<u>**EVEN ON MY DARK DAYS**</u>

Even on my dark days, your love poems I'll write,

Even on my dark days, I just want to be your mister right.

Even on my dark days, for you I'll always afford a smile,

Even on my dark days, I'll always love you.

<u>**GIVE ME A REASON TO HATE YOU**</u>

If you badly want me to go,

Then give me a reason to do so.

There's nothing about you that I know,

That would make me say NO.

If you badly want me to go,

Then give me a reason to hate you.

<u>**I CHOOSE ME OVER YOU**</u>

I can do anything for us,

But not at the expense of my life.

I love you enough to die for you,

But I won't end my life because of us.

Not everything was meant to work,

So, if this won't, then so be it.

I love you so much you know I do,

But I choose me over you.

<u>WHEN I LOVE</u>

When I love, I forget me,

When I love, that's how I be.

When I love, me turns to we,

When I love, that's how I be.

When I love, I give it my all,

When I love, that's how I be.

When I love, that's how I be.

MY SOUL IS BLEEDING

It's like cancer, spreading throughout my heart,

So much pain, it deeply hurts.

My heart is in pain,

I don't want this, not again.

I don't want this, not again.

My body is aching,

My mind is unstable,

And my soul is bleeding.

I'M NOT A ROCK

In my veins, there's blood,

In my chest, there's a chest.

Within my body there's a soul.

Love me right or not,

I'd want you to know this,

I'm not a rock.

I'M NOT PERFECT BUT I'LL TRY

Under the sun and over the sky,

There's no one like you, that I know.

You deserve the best,

And I'll give you my best.

But one thing you should know my love,

Is that I'm not perfect but I'll try.